States

MASSACHUSETTS

by Jordan Mills

CAPSTONE PRESS
a capstone imprint

Next Page Books are published by Capstone Press,
1710 Roe Crest Drive, North Mankato, Minnesota 56003
www.mycapstone.com

Library of Congress Cataloging-in-Publication Data
Cataloging-in-publication information is on file with the Library of
Congress.
ISBN 978-1-5157-0408-9 (library binding)
ISBN 978-1-5157-0467-6 (paperback)
ISBN 978-1-5157-0519-2 (ebook PDF)

Editorial Credits
Jaclyn Jaycox, editor; Richard Korab and Katy LaVigne, designers;
Morgan Walters, media researcher; Laura Manthe, production specialist

Photo Credits
Capstone Press: Angi Gahler, map 4, 7; Corbis: Sygma/James
Andanson, middle 19; Library of Congress: Prints and Photographs
Division, middle 18, bottom 18, bottom 19, 27; One Mile Up, Inc.,
23; Shutterstock: AHPix, 14, Andrew F. Kazmierski, 6, AR Pictures,
11, B. Speckart, middle right 21, Bildagentur Zoonar GmbH, bottom
right 21, Denis Tabler, bottom right 20, Everett Historical, 12, 26, 28,
f11photo, 16, 17, fmua, 29, Georgios Kollidas, top 18, holbox, 5, Jeff
Banke, middle left 21, Jeffrey M. Frank, 7, jiawangkun, bottom left
8, Lenka_N, top right 21, Marcio Jose Bastos Silva, bottom right 8,
10, Mayabuns, top right 20, MVPhoto, bottom left 20, s_bukley, top
19, schankz, top 24, Sean Pavone, 25, Songquan Deng, bottom 24,
StepanPopov, 15, Suchan, 9, Sunny Chanruangvanich, cover, Vlada Z,
top left 21, Zack Frank, 13; Wikimedia: Didier Descouens, bottom left
21, Matt Lavin, top left 20

All design elements by Shutterstock

Printed and bound in China.
0316/CA21600187
012016 009436F16

TABLE OF CONTENTS

Want to take your research further? Ask your librarian if your school subscribes to PebbleGo Next. If so, when you see this helpful symbol ☞ throughout the book, log onto www.pebblegonext.com for bonus downloads and information.

LOCATION

Massachusetts is in the northeastern United States. The Atlantic Ocean makes up the state's east coast. Cape Cod forms a hook that juts into the Atlantic Ocean. Connecticut and Rhode Island border Massachusetts to the south. To the west is New York. Vermont and New Hampshire lie to the north. Boston is Massachusetts' capital and largest city. The state's next largest cities are Worcester and Springfield.

PebbleGo Next Bonus!
To print and label your own map, go to www.pebblegonext.com and search keywords:
MA MAP

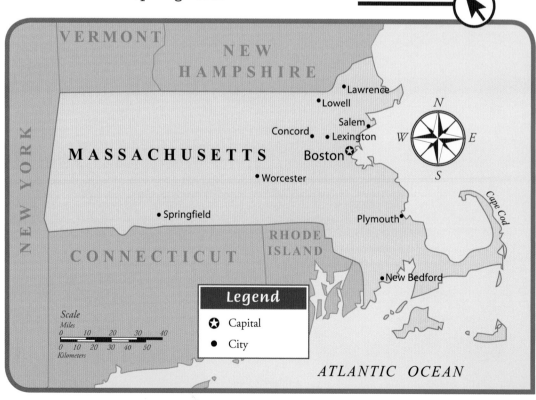

VERMONT

NEW HAMPSHIRE

NEW YORK

MASSACHUSETTS

• Lawrence
• Lowell
Salem•
Concord• • Lexington
Boston ✪
• Worcester

• Springfield

Plymouth•

Cape Cod

RHODE ISLAND

CONNECTICUT

• New Bedford

N
W   E
S

Legend
✪ Capital
• City

Scale
Miles
0   10   20   30   40
0   10   20   30   40   50
Kilometers

ATLANTIC OCEAN

Boston has a population of 645,966.

GEOGRAPHY

Western Massachusetts has rolling hills. The Berkshire Mountains have the state's highest peaks. Mount Greylock, at 3,487 feet (1,063 meters) above sea level, is the state's highest point.

In the middle of the state is the Quabbin Reservoir. It covers 39 square miles (101 square kilometers) in the middle of the state. Quabbin supplies drinking water for the Boston area.

The eastern part of the state has many islands, including Martha's Vineyard, Nantucket Island, and the Elizabeth Islands. Many spots along the coast are rocky, but some areas have wide, sandy beaches. Cape Cod draws thousands of visitors each year to its beautiful beaches.

PebbleGo Next Bonus! To watch a video about the Pilgrim Hall Museum, go to www.pebblegonext.com and search keywords:

MA VIDEO

Martha's Vineyard is located south of Cape Cod.

Visitors can see 60 to 90 miles (97 to 145 km) from the top of Mount Greylock.

BERKSHIRE MOUNTAINS

▲ Mount Greylock

Connecticut River

Quabbin Reservoir

Massachusetts Bay

Cape Cod

Cape Cod Bay

Assawompset Pond

Nantucket Island

Elizabeth Islands

Martha's Vineyard

Legend

▲ Highest Point

◯ Lake

⛰ Mountain Range

〜 River

Scale
Miles
0   10   20   30   40

0   10   20   30   40   50
Kilometers

ATLANTIC OCEAN

WEATHER

Massachusetts has warm summers and cold winters. The average summer temperature is 68 degrees Fahrenheit (20 degrees Celsius). The average winter temperature is 27°F (-3°C).

Average High and Low Temperatures (Boston, MA)

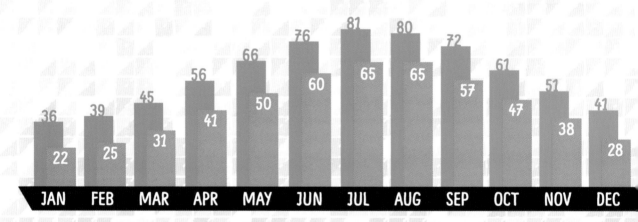

JAN	FEB	MAR	APR	MAY	JUN	JUL	AUG	SEP	OCT	NOV	DEC
36	39	45	56	66	76	81	80	72	61	51	41
22	25	31	41	50	60	65	65	57	47	38	28

LANDMARKS

Plimoth Plantation

Plimoth Plantation is a museum that shows what the original Plymouth Colony was like. Volunteers re-create what life was like in 1627. Exhibits tell the stories of both the English colonists and the American Indians.

Plymouth Rock

Plymouth Rock is the symbolic stepping-stone where the Pilgrims first set foot on land in what became Plymouth Colony. Even though there is no historical proof that the Pilgrims actually stepped on this rock, nearly 1 million people each year come from all over the world to visit the boulder.

Martha's Vineyard

Martha's Vineyard is an island off the southeastern coast of Massachusetts. The island is a famous summer vacation spot. It has pleasant summer weather and beautiful beaches.

The Pilgrims and American Indians celebrated the first Thanksgiving in 1621.

In 1620 Pilgrims from England arrived at Plymouth, in what is now Massachusetts. Wampanoag American Indian chief Massasoit and his people taught the settlers to grow corn, which helped the colonists survive. Over time more people from England settled in Massachusetts.

American colonists began protesting British rule and high taxes. On December 16, 1773, they sneaked onto a British ship and dumped tea into Boston Harbor to protest a tax on tea. This event was called the Boston Tea Party.

In 1775 the first battles of the Revolutionary War, the Battles of Lexington and Concord, took place in Massachusetts. After the colonists won the war, Massachusetts became the sixth state in 1788.

The Massachusetts legislature makes the state's laws. Its official name is the General Court. It includes the 40-member Senate and 160-member House of Representatives. The governor is the leader of the executive branch. The courts and judges make up the judicial branch.

The state capitol building is located in Boston.

INDUSTRY

Many industries contribute to Massachusetts' economy. The state has a variety of farm products. Farmers raise fruits, vegetables, and nursery products. Farmers also raise dairy cattle, poultry, hogs, and sheep. Only Wisconsin produces more cranberries than Massachusetts. Fishers catch lobster, clams, cod, herring, crabs, and other fish and shellfish. Fishers in New Bedford on the state's southeastern coast catch half the scallops sold in the United States.

Massachusetts is a leading center of technological and

Massachusetts is one of the leading commercial fishing states.

medical equipment. Companies in the state make computers and computer parts.

Higher education is important to Massachusetts. The state is home to more than 100 colleges.

Many tourists travel to famous Massachusetts historical locations. Tourists also visit the state's beautiful beaches, especially those on Cape Cod, Nantucket, and Martha's Vineyard.

Cranberry harvest season runs from September through November.

POPULATION

People have come to Massachusetts from all over the world. During the 1850s many Irish immigrants settled in South Boston. Italian immigrants settled in Boston's North End and in Revere. Portuguese fishermen brought their skills and families to Gloucester, New Bedford, and Fall River.

The next largest ethnic group is the fast-growing Hispanic population. Many Puerto Rican, Dominicans, and natives of Central and South America have moved to Lawrence and Lowell.

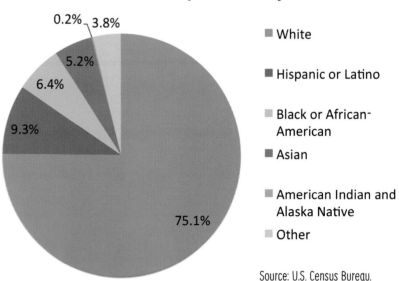

Population by Ethnicity

0.2% 3.8%
5.2%
6.4%
9.3%
75.1%

- White
- Hispanic or Latino
- Black or African-American
- Asian
- American Indian and Alaska Native
- Other

Source: U.S. Census Bureau.

African-Americans have always been a part of Massachusetts. They make up about 6 percent of the state's population.

More than 5 percent of people in the state are of Asian descent. Asian immigrants have long been an important part of Massachusetts. Chinatown is one of Boston's thriving neighborhoods.

FAMOUS PEOPLE

Benjamin Franklin (1706–1790) was an author, inventor, and colonial leader. He was born in Boston.

John F. Kennedy (1917–1963) was the 35th U.S. president (1961–1963). He was born in Brookline. Kennedy also served Massachusetts in the U.S. House of Representatives (1947–1953) and the Senate (1953–1961). While president, he was shot and killed in Dallas, Texas.

Paul Revere (1735–1818) was born in Boston. He took part in the Boston Tea Party, but he is best known for his midnight ride. The night before the Battles of Lexington and Concord, he warned people that British troops were coming.

Matt Damon (1970–) is a famous movie actor and Academy Award–winning writer. His movies include the *Bourne Identity* series and *We Bought a Zoo*. He grew up in Cambridge.

Richard Scarry (1919–1994) was a children's book author and illustrator of more than 300 books. His first famous book *Richard Scarry's Best Word Book Ever* was published in 1963. He grew up in Boston.

Dr. Seuss (1904–1991) was born Theodor Seuss Geisel in Springfield. His rhyming books are beloved by generations, including *The Cat in the Hat* and *Green Eggs and Ham*.

STATE SYMBOLS

Tree

American elm

Flower

mayflower

Bird

chickadee

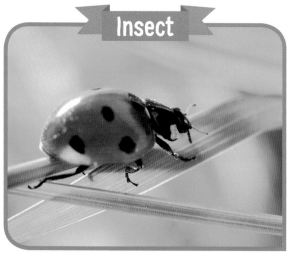

Insect

ladybug

PebbleGo Next Bonus! To make a famous Ruth Wakefield dessert, go to www.pebblegonext.com and search keywords:

MA RECIPE

Fish

cod

Dog

Boston terrier

Game Bird

wild turkey

Horse

Morgan horse

Mineral

babingtonite

Marine Mammal

right whale

FAST FACTS

STATEHOOD
1788

CAPITAL ☆
Boston

LARGEST CITY ●
Boston

SIZE
7,800 square miles (20,202 square kilometers) land area
(2010 U.S. Census Bureau)

POPULATION
6,692,824 (2013 U.S. Census estimate)

STATE NICKNAME
Bay State

STATE MOTTO
"By the sword we seek peace, but peace only under liberty"

STATE SEAL

The state seal includes Massachusetts' coat of arms in a circle. The arm with a sword illustrates the state motto, "By the sword we seek peace, but peace only under liberty." The motto represents the state's key role in the Revolutionary War. The seal was made official on June 4, 1885.

PebbleGo Next Bonus! To print and color your own flag, go to www.pebblegonext.com and search keywords:

MA FLAG

STATE FLAG

Massachusetts' flag shows the state's coat of arms on a white background. An American Indian on the shield holds a bow and an arrow. The arrow is pointed downward to stand for peace. The white star shows that Massachusetts was one of the 13 original American colonies. The current flag was adopted in 1971.

MINING PRODUCTS

sand and gravel, traprock, granite, dimension stone

MANUFACTURED GOODS

computer and electronic products, metal products, chemicals

FARM PRODUCTS

nursery plants, dairy products, cranberries, vegetables, poultry

PROFESSIONAL SPORTS TEAMS

Boston Red Sox (MLB)
New England Revolution (MLS)
Boston Celtics (NBA)
New England Patriots (NFL)
Boston Bruins (NHL)

PebbleGo Next Bonus!
To learn the lyrics to
the state song, go to
www.pebblegonext.com
and search keywords:

MA SONG

MASSACHUSETTS TIMELINE

1500s Thousands of American Indians are living in the area that is now Massachusetts.

1620 The Pilgrims establish a colony in the New World in present-day Massachusetts.

1621 The first Thanksgiving is celebrated in Plymouth.

1636 Harvard, the oldest college in the United States, opens in Cambridge.

1675–1676 The colonists defeat Wampanoag Chief King Philip in the battle known as King Philip's War.

1692 The Salem Witch Trials take place. Mostly out of fear, people accuse others of using witchcraft to cause illnesses. Twenty people are executed as witches.

1770 Tensions between British soldiers and the colonists lead to a fight on a Boston street on March 5. British soldiers kill five colonists. Later known as the Boston Massacre, the event angers the colonists and soon helps bring about the Revolutionary War.

1773 On December 16 Boston colonists dump tea into Boston Harbor to protest Britain's tea tax; the event becomes known as the Boston Tea Party.

1775 The Battles of Lexington and Concord start the Revolutionary War on April 19.

1788 Massachusetts becomes the sixth state on February 6.

1796 John Adams of Quincy is elected the country's second president.

1815 The state's first textile mill opens in Lowell.

1820 On March 15 Maine separates from Massachusetts to become its own state.

1824 John Quincy Adams of Braintree is elected the sixth president; he was the son of John Adams.

1861–1865 The Union and the Confederacy fight the Civil War; Massachusetts fights for the Union.

1876 Alexander Graham Bell demonstrates the first telephone in Boston.

1914–1918 World War I is fought; the United States enters the war in 1917.

1939–1945 World War II is fought; the United States enters the war in 1941.

1960
John F. Kennedy from Brookline is elected president; he is the youngest president ever elected.

1988
Massachusetts celebrates its 200th anniversary as a state.

2001
Jane Swift becomes the youngest female governor in U.S. history.

2013
During the Boston Marathon on April 15, two bombs explode, killing three people and injuring 264.

2015
Boston is shut down due to a blizzard that affects up to 60 million people in the northeast.

Glossary

contribute *(kuhn-TRI-byoot)*—to offer help to a group or organization

economy *(i-KON-uh-mee)*—the ways in which a country handles its money and resources

ethnicity *(ETH-niss-ih-tee)*—a group of people who share the same physical features, beliefs, and backgrounds

executive *(ig-ZE-kyuh-tiv)*—the branch of government that makes sure laws are followed

exhibit *(ig-ZI-buht)*—a display that shows something to the public

immigrant *(IM-uh-gruhnt)*—someone who comes from abroad to live permanently in a country

industry *(IN-duh-stree)*—a business which produces a product or provides a service

legislature *(LEJ-iss-lay-chur)*—a group of elected officials who have the power to make or change laws for a country or state

region *(REE-juhn)*—a large area

reservoir *(REZ-uh-vwar)*—a natural or artificial holding area for storing a large amount of water

symbolic *(sim-BAHL-ic)*—representing, or standing for, something else

Read More

Bjorklund, Ruth. *Massachusetts: the Bay State*. It's My State! New York: Cavendish Square Publishing, 2015.

Ganeri, Anita. *United States of America: A Benjamin Blog and His Inquisitive Dog Guide*. Country Guides. Chicago: Heinemann Raintree, 2015.

Lanser, Amanda. *What's Great About Massachusetts?* Our Great States. Minneapolis: Lerner Publications Company, 2015.

Internet Sites

FactHound offers a safe, fun way to find Internet sites related to this book. All of the sites on FactHound have been researched by our staff.

Here's all you do:

Visit *www.facthound.com*

Type in this code: 9781515704089

 Check out projects, games and lots more at
www.capstonekids.com

Critical Thinking Using the Common Core

1. Plymouth Rock is one of three state landmarks in Massachusetts. What are the other two? (Key Ideas and Details)

2. Many Revolutionary War Events happened in Massachusetts. Why do you think this is important for its tourism industry? (Integration of Knowledge and Ideas)

3. What ethnicity is 9.3 percent of Massachusetts population? Use the pie chart on page 16 for help. (Craft and Structure)

Index